Know Your Emotions

ANGRY IS ...

by Connie Colwell Miller

CAPSTONE PRESS
a capstone imprint

Anger ties you up in knots.
It winds your muscles tight.
Your eyes are dark. Your face is scrunched.
Your insides don't feel right.

3

"Clean your room," your parents say.
"This mess has got to go!"
You like your room the way it is!
Your anger starts to grow.

4

5

Mistakes are sure to happen,
and sometimes life seems bad.
Your dog might eat your ice cream cone
and, boy, that makes you mad!

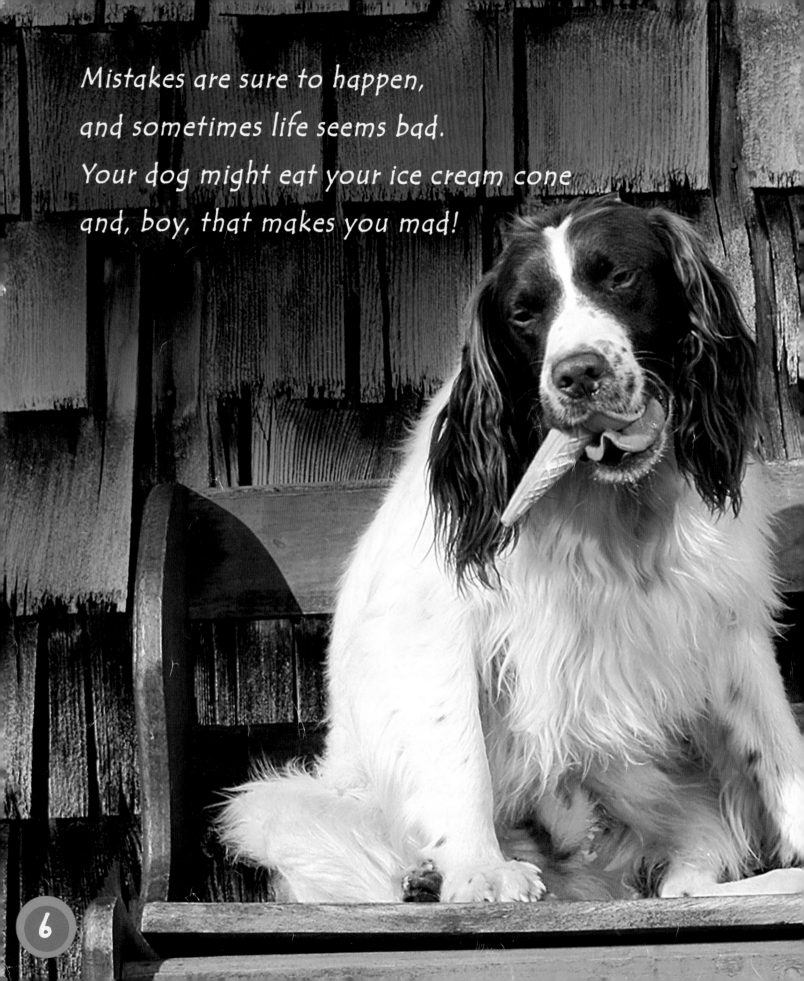

You let a friend play with your toy.
She broke it right in two.
Anger fills you up inside,
and you're not sure what to do.

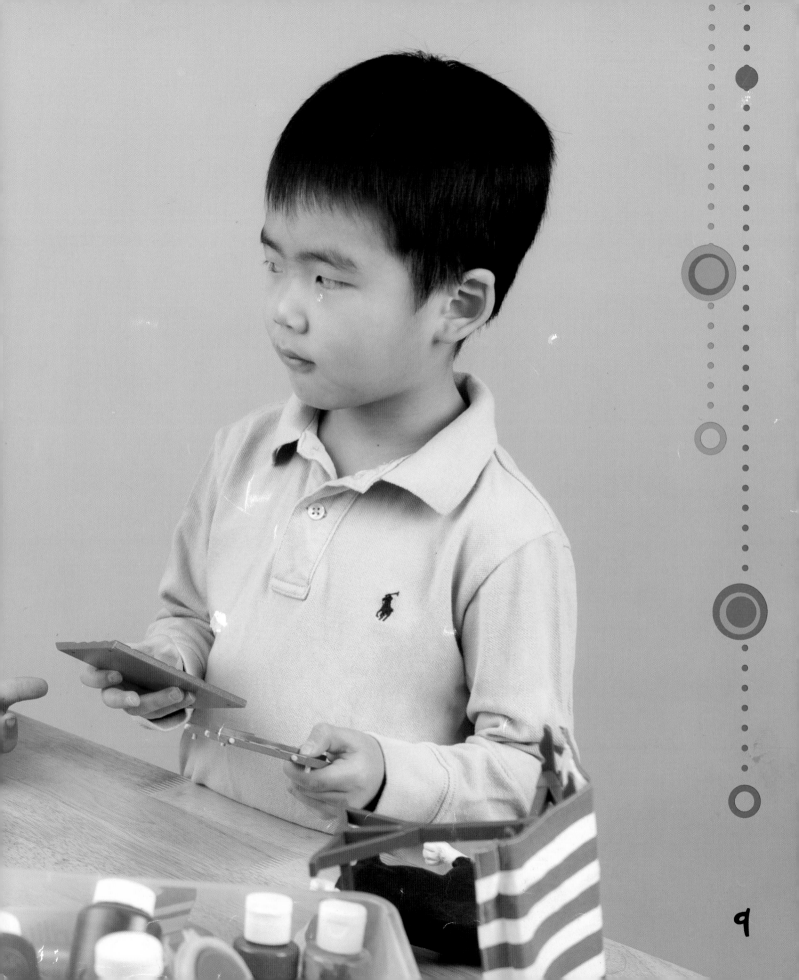

You just can't stand steamed broccoli!
It never tasted great.
You want to shout and stomp your feet
when mom says, "Clean your plate!"

11

Oops! It slipped—a no-no word
you didn't mean to say.
You felt bad, but now you're mad—
you're grounded for the day!

13

On the couch, you get so mad—
your brother makes a face.
He sits too close. He bothers you.
He won't give you your space!

15

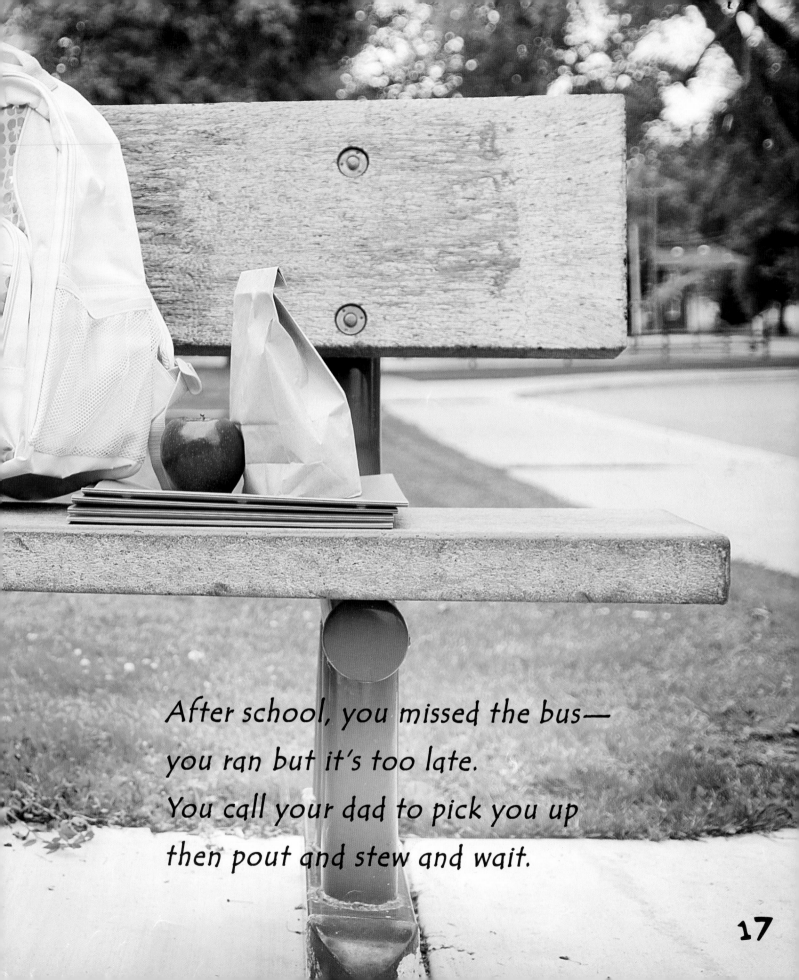

After school, you missed the bus—
you ran but it's too late.
You call your dad to pick you up
then pout and stew and wait.

Anger's racing in your mind—
you need to let it out.
Find a place where it is safe
to scream or cry or shout.

19

It's true we all get mad sometimes.
We feel it now and then.
But when it grows, just let it go—
you'll feel like you again!

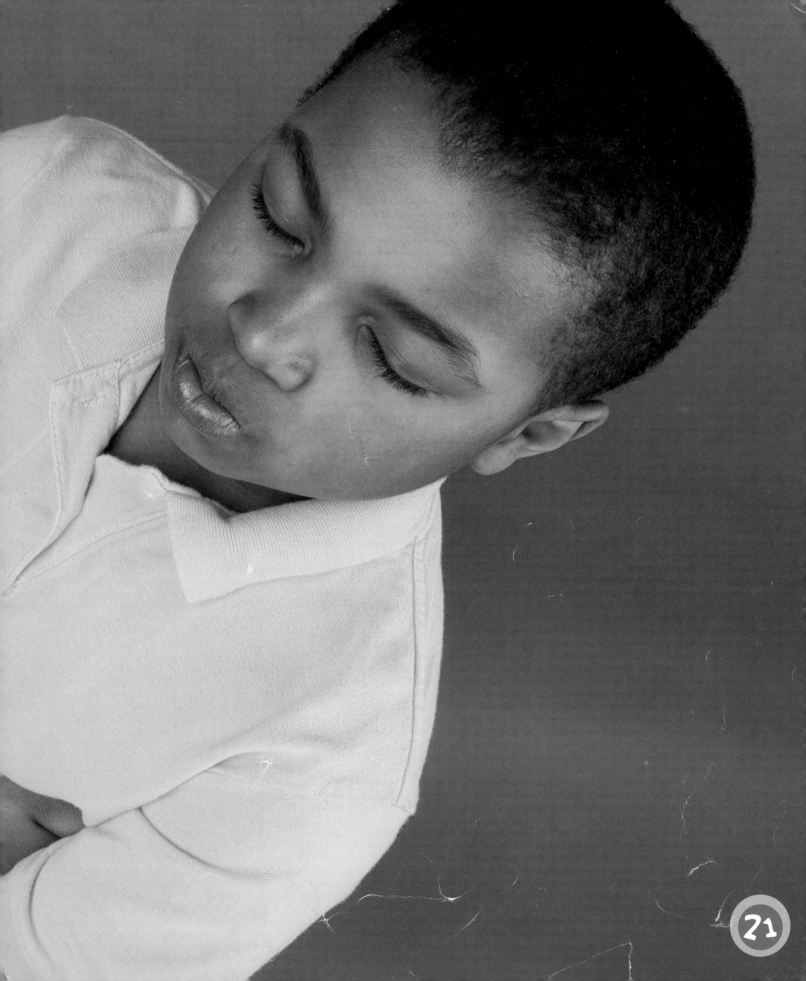

21

GLOSSARY

ground—to punish someone by not allowing them to leave

pout—to push out your lips when you are angry or disappointed about something

race—to run or move very fast

scrunch—to squish together

stew—to worry about something or think about it a lot

READ MORE

Meister, Cari. *Everyone Feels Angry Sometimes.* Everyone Has Feelings. MInneapolis: Picture Window Books, 2010.

Snow, Todd, and Peggy Snow. *Feelings to Share from A to Z.* Oak Park Heights, Minn.: Maren Green, 2007.

Wagenbach, Debbie. *The Grouchies.* Washington D. C.: Magination Press, 2010.

Internet Sites

FactHound offers a safe, fun way to find Internet sites related to this book. All of the sites on FactHound have been researched by our staff.

Here's all you do:

Visit *www.facthound.com*

Type in this code: 9781429660440

Check out projects, games and lots more at **www.capstonekids.com**

Index

A+ Books are published by Capstone Press,
151 Good Counsel Drive, P.O. Box 669, Mankato, Minnesota 56002.
www.capstonepub.com

Books published by Capstone Press are manufactured with paper
containing at least 10 percent post-consumer waste.

Library of Congress Cataloging-in-Publication Data
Miller, Connie Colwell, 1976–
  Angry is... / by Connie Colwell Miller.
    p. cm.—(A+ books. Know your emotions)
  Includes bibliographical references and index.
  Summary: "Photographs and short rhyming verses describe how it feels to be angry"—Provided by publisher.
  ISBN 978-1-4296-6044-0 (library binding) ISBN 978-1-4296-7044-9 (paperback)
  1. Anger in children—Juvenile literature. 2. Anger—Juvenile literature. 3. Emotions in children—Juvenile literature. I. Title.
II. Series.

  BF723.A4M55 2012
  152.4'7—dc22   2011006128

Credits

Jeni Wittrock, editor; Alison Thiele, designer; Svetlana Zhurkin, media researcher; Sarah Schuette, photo stylist;
    Marcy Morin; studio scheduler; Eric Manske, production specialist

Photo Credits

Capstone Studio/Karon Dubke, 1, 4–5, 8–9, 12–13, 14–15, 20–21
iStockphoto/Bonnie Jacobs, 10–11; Chris Fertnig, 6–7; Leigh Schindler, cover; Rosemarie Gearhart, 16–17
Shutterstock/Benjamin Haas, 18–19; JPagetRFphotos, 2–3

Note to Parents, Teachers, and Librarians

This Know Your Emotions book uses full color photographs and a nonfiction format to introduce the concept of
being angry. *Angry Is...* is designed to be read aloud to a pre-reader or to be read independently by an early reader.
Photographs help listeners and early readers understand the text and concepts discussed. The book encourages further
learning by including the following sections: Glossary, Read More, Internet Sites, Index. Early readers may need assistance
using these features.

4733 9303 11/11

Printed in the United States of America in North Mankato, Minnesota.
032011   006110CGF11